AIM~~ING FOR~~

782.42
IRV

The Library & Learning Centre
Abingdon Campus
Wootton Road
Abingdon OX14 1GG
01235 216240
library@abingdon-witney.ac.uk

<u>**This book is due for return on or before the last**</u>
<u>**date shown below.**</u>

Andy Irvine

AIMING FOR THE HEART

Irish Song Affairs

Illustrationen
Eamonn O'Doherty
Intro
Paul Brady

Song Bücherei

Revidierte Ausgabe
2. Auflage 2008
Übersetzungen: Rainer Schobeß
Copyright © by Heupferd Musik Verlag GmbH, Dreieich
Alle Rechte vorbehalten / all rights reserved
Die Song Bücherei wird herausgegeben von
Christian Winkelmann
und erscheint im Heupferd Musik Verlag
www.heupferd-musik.de
Text- & Notensatz: Y & M
Printed in Germany
ISBN 978-3-923445-05-9

Contents / Inhalt

Intro 6
West Coast Of Clare 8
Arthur MacBride 11
Pat Reilly 14
Time Will Cure Me 16
Plains Of Kildare 20
Bonny Woodhall 22
Martinmas Time 24
Autumn Gold 28
The Rambling Siúler 31
You Rambling Boys Of Pleasure 34
Smeceno Horo 36
Roger O'Hehir 38
Kellswater 40
Johnny Of Brady's Lea 44
Thousands Are Sailing 47
Napoleon Bonaparte 49
General Monroe 51
Farewell To Old Ireland 53
Edward Connors 57
The Longford Weaver 59
Farewell To Ballymoney 62
Romanian Song (Blood And Gold) 64
King Bore And The Sandman 66
Rainy Sundays 68
Willy O'Winsbury 72
Creggan White Hare 75
At Twenty-One 78
Captain Colston 81
Captain Thunderbolt 83
The Dodger's Song 86
Baneasa's Green Glade 90
Sure To Be A Row 92
My Heart's Tonight In Ireland 94
Outro 98
The Works / Die Werke 101
Discography 104
Those were the days 105

Intro

The moment I first heard Andy Irvine, one foggy Autumn evening in O'Meara's pub on Dublin's Aston's Quay, I knew I was listening to something very special. It was 1966 and a time when most other singers of the day were contriving to sound either like the Clancy Brothers or the Dubliners. But here was someone who sang with a voice that was truly original, a style that owed nothing to the cliched „Irish Ballad Singer" style that was developing even then and which has become, to this listeners ears at least, so tedious over the years.

Among this rapidly developing morass of mediocrity, Andy Irvine's voice stood out like a welcoming light, a warm fire on a winter's night. This warmth and integrity has remained with him ever since.

But Andy's singing is only half of the story. His harmonica playing and ready facility with almost any stringed instrument led him from his earlier days with „Sweeney's Men" to become one of the cornerstones of the legendary „Planxty" sound - a sound which, throughout the seventies, gradually and permanently changed the way the world looked at Irish music.

Nevertheless, all this talent would have amounted to little were it not for Andy's „ear for a good song". Few singers over the past years can claim to have brought to the attention of listeners such a wealth of classic and beautiful songs - and not only those traditional tunes he painstakingly researched and lovingly arranged but also his own compositions.

The best of his early songs are now collected together in this book and not before time. If you the reader, can derive one tenth of the pleasure from it that I have - well then your money will have been well spent.

Good singing and happy reading!

Paul Brady

In dem Moment als ich Andy Irvine zum ersten Mal hörte - es war an einem nebligen Herbstabend in O'Meara's Pub am Aston's Quay in Dublin - wußte ich, daß ich etwas ganz Besonderem lauschte. Das war 1966 und zu einer Zeit, als die meisten anderen Sänger all ihren Erfindungsreichtum daran setzten, so wie die „Clancy Brothers" oder aber wie die „Dubliners" zu klingen. Doch hier war jemand, der mit einer wahrhaft originären Stimme sang, auf eine Art, die in nichts dem klischeehaften Stil des „Irischen Balladensängers" verpflichtet war, welcher sich damals gerade herausbildete und im Laufe der Jahre, zumindest für den Verfasser dieser Zeilen, so ermüdend wurde.

Mitten aus dem sich rasch ausbreitenden Sumpf der Mittelmäßigkeit ragte Andy Irvines Stimme heraus wie ein freundliches Licht, wie ein wärmendes Feuer an einem frostigen Winterabend. Diese Ausstrahlung und Integrität sind ihm seither geblieben.

Dabei ist Andys Gesang nur eine Seite der Medaille. Sein Harmonica-Spiel, besonders aber seine virtuose Beherrschung fast aller Saiteninstrumente ließen ihn nach seinen frühen Tagen mit „Sweeney's Men" zu einem Eckpfeiler des legendären „Planxty"-Sounds werden. Eines Sounds, der während der 70er Jahre allmählich doch stetig das Erscheinungsbild der irischen Musik in den Augen der Welt veränderte.

Dennoch hätten all diese Talente nur wenig gezählt, wäre da nicht Andys besonderes Gespür für die Qualitäten eines Liedes gewesen. Nur wenige Sänger der vergangenen Jahre können für sich in Anspruch nehmen, dem Publikum solch eine Fülle alter und schöner Lieder nahegebracht zu haben. Dies gilt nicht nur für traditionelle Melodien, die er hingebungsvoll erkundete und mit Liebe bearbeitete, sondern auch für seine eigenen Kompositionen.

Die besten seiner frühen Lieder sind nun in diesem Buch vereint und das bestimmt nicht zu früh. Wenn Ihnen, verehrter Leser, diese Sammlung auch nur halb so viel Freude bereitet, wie mir, dann dürfte es mit Sicherheit eine passable Anlage sein.

Viel Vergnügen beim Singen und Lesen!

Paul Brady

West Coast Of Clare

Words & Music: Andy Irvine

There'a always a slightly sad and lonely feeling, returning to a place after a mighty event. Sitting in a now empty pub or walking through a once crowded street, vivid with memories. The setting for this song was the Fleadh Cheoil in Kilrush in 1965 followed by further mayhem in Milltown Malbay. I started the song in County Clare and finished it in Ljubljana, Slovenia, in 1968.

Kehrt man an einen Ort zurück, an dem Entscheidendes geschehen ist, so stellt sich immer ein leichtes Gefühl von Einsamkeit und Trauer ein. Beim Bier in einer nun leeren Kneipe oder beim Schlendern durch eine einst belebte Straße kommen dann lebhafte Erinnerungen auf. Dieses Lied entstand vor dem Hintergrund des Fleadh Cheoil (Nationaler irischer Wettbewerb für traditionelles Instrumentalspiel; Anm. d. Übers.) von 1965 in Kilrush, dem großer Katzenjammer in Milltown Malbay folgte. Begonnen habe ich es im County Clare, beendet 1968 in Ljubljana, Slovenien.

Sorrow and sadness, bitterness, grief
Memories I have of you, won't leave me in peace
My mind was running back to the West Coast of Clare
Thinking of you and the times we had there.

I walked to Spanish Point, I knew I'd find you there
I stood on the White Strand and you were everywhere
Vivid memories fade but the mood still remains
I wish I could go back and be with you again.

In Milltown there's a pub, it's there and I sit down
I see you everywhere your face is all around
The search for times past, contains such sweet pain
I'll banish lonesome thoughts but they'll return again.

I walk along the shore, the rain in my face
My mind is numb with grief, of you there is no trace
I'll think of this again, when in far off lands I roam
Walking with you by this cold Atlantic foam.

Sorrow and sadness, bitterness, grief
Memories I have of you, won't leave me in peace
My mind was running back to the West Coast of Clare
Thinking of you and the times we had there.

Arthur MacBride

Words & Music: trad., arr. Andy Irvine

This famous song would appear to me to have originated in Donegal or in Scotland. It's popularity was such that it travelled to England and America and has been recorded by Martin Carthy, Paul Brady and „Planxty" to name but a few. The Recruiting Sergeant and his party must have been a curse to the common people of Ireland at the time of the Napleonic wars, especially as most of them would have had more sympathy with Napoleon than with the British.

Dieses berühmte Lied scheint mir in Donegal oder in Scottland entstanden zu sein. Es war bekannt, daß es bis nach England und Amerika gelangte. Aufgenommen wurde es von Martin Carthy, Paul Brady und von „Planxty", um nur einige zu nennen. Der Werbeoffizier und seine Leute müssen zur Zeit der Napoleonischen Kriege ein Fluch für das einfache Volk in Irland gewesen sein, zumal die meisten Iren mehr Sympathien für Napoleon als für die Briten gehegt haben dürften.

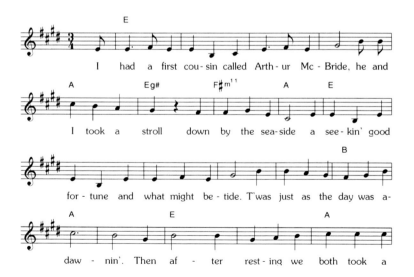

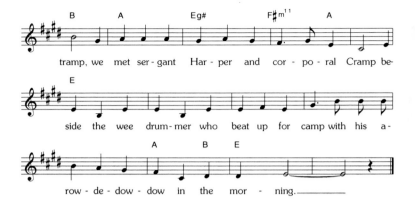

tramp, we met ser - gant Har - per and cor - po - ral Cramp be-
side the wee drum - mer who beat up for camp with his a-
row - de - dow - dow in the mor - ning.

I had a first cousin called Arthur MacBride
He and I took a stroll down by the seaside
A seekin' good fortune and what might betide
T'was after restin' we both took a tramp
We met sergeant Harper and corporal Cramp
Besides the wee drummer who beat up for camp
With his row de dow dow in the morning.

He says me young fellows if you will enlist
A guinea you quickly will get in your first
Besides a crown for to kick up the dust
And drink the King's health in the morning
For a soldier he leads a very fine life
And he always is blessed with a charming young wife
And he pays all his debts without sorrow or strife
And always lives happy and charming.

And a soldier he always is decent and clean
In the finest of clothing he's constantly seen
While other poor fellows go dirty and mean
And sup on thin gruel in the morning
Says Arthur I wouldn't be proud of your clothes
For you've only the lend of them as I suppose
And you dare not change them one night for you know
If you do you'll be flogged in the morning.

And although we are single and free
We take great delight in our own company
And we have no desire strange countries to see
Although that your offer is charming
And we have no desire to take your advance
All hazards and dangers we barter on chance
And you'd have no scruple but to send us to France
Where we would be shot without warning.

Ah now says the sergeant if I hear but one word
I instantly now will out with my sword
And into your bodies as strength will afford
So now my gay devils take warning
But Arthur and I, we took the odds we gave them no chance
For to launch out their swords
Our whackin' shillelaghs came over their heads
And paid them right smart in the morning.

As for the wee drummer we rifeled his pow
And we made a football of his row de dow dow
And into the ocean to rock and row
And bid it a tedious returning
As for the old rapier that hung by his side
We flung it as far as we could in the tide
„To the Devil I pitch you", says Arthur MacBride,
„To temper your Steel in the morning".

Pat Reilly

Words & Music: trad., arr. Andy Irvine

The other side of the coin. There's many's the song tells this tale, of the hard working man, taking a drink after his day's work, meeting the recruiting sergeant and waking up on the parade ground with a violent hangover. This song is found in many different versions in the North of Ireland. I have another version called „The Black Horse".

Die Kehrseite der Medaille. So manches Lied erzählt die Geschichte des Mannes, der nach seinem schweren Tagwerk ein Glas trinkt, den Werbeoffizier trifft und schließlich mit einem gewaltigen Kater auf dem Exerzierplatz wieder aufwacht. Von diesem Lied finden sich viele verschiedene Varianten in Nordirland. Ich habe eine weitere Fassung „The Black Horse" benannt.

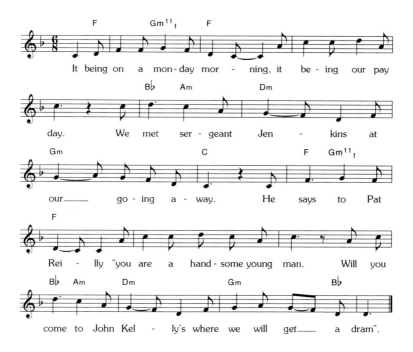

It being on a monday morning, it being our pay day
We met Sergeant Jenkins at our going away
He says to Pat Reilly: You are a handsome young man
Will you come to John Kelly's where we will get a dram.

And while we sat there boozing and drinking our dram
He says to Pat Reilly: You are a handsome young man
I'd have you take the bounty and come along with me
To the sweet County Longford strange faces for to see.

O no kind sir a soldiers life me would not agree
Nor neither would I bind myself down from liberty
For I lived as happy as a prince my mind does tell me so
So fare you well I'm just going down my shuttle for to throw.

O it's I took the bounty the reckoning was paid
The ribbons were brought out me boys and pinned to my cockade
It's early the next morning we alle were made to stand
Before our grand General with hats all in our hands.

He says to Pat Reilly: you are a little to low
With some other regiment I fear you'll have to go
I may go where I will I have no one to mourn
For my mother is dead me boys and never will return.

It's not in the morning that I sing my song
But it's in the cold evening as I march alone
With my gun o'er my shoulder I bitterly do weep
When I think of my true love now lies fast asleep.

My blessing on my mother who reared me neat and clean
But bad luck to my father who made me serve the Queen
O had he been an honest man and learned me my trade
I would never have listed nor worn the cockade.

Time Will Cure Me

Words & Music: Andy Irvine

This is one of a series of four songs I wrote while on my travels in Eastern Europe in 1968 and 1969. The girl was from Israel where a type of cactus called „Sabra" grows, hence „Sabra Girl". Suffice it to say that time did cure my aching heart! The song was recorded by „Planxty" in 1973 on the album „The Well below the Valley".

Eines von vier Liedern, die ich 1968 und 1989 während meiner Reise durch Osteuropa geschrieben habe. Das besungene Mädchen stammte aus Israel, wo eine Kaktusart namens „Sabra" wächst. Daher nannte ich sie „Sabra-Mädchen". Es genügt zu sagen, daß die Zeit wirklich mein wundes Herz geheilt hat. Das Lied wurde 1973 von „Planxty" für das Album „The Well below the Valley" aufgenommen.

17

Lonely, the life that once I led
Strange the paths on which we tread
Led me to you unlikely but true
Sabra girl, clouding my view.

Rainy, the day, the first time we met
Deep was the talk as we lay on your bed
It didn't seem wrong to sing a sad song
Sabra girl, soon you'd be gone.

Early the morning and sad the goodbye
With a wave of your hand and a smile of your eye
So lately did meet, no sooner to part
Sabra girl, homeward must start.

Rosy, the lines that you wrote with your hand
Reading between them to misunderstand
I made the mistake
You said not to make

Yes reading your letters conviction did grow
I thought it a chance and I knew I must go
It's hard to believe I could be so naive
Sabra girl, flattered but to deceive.

And now you just told me that friendship is all
I'm forced to repair the breach in my wall
Illusions and dreams as usual it seems
Sabra girl, they have been my downfall.

Lonely the life and dismal the view
Closed, the road that leads to you
Since better can't be as friends we'll agree
Sabra girl, time will cure me.

Plains Of Kildare

New Words & Music: Andy Irvine

Stewball or Skewball was a remarkable horse. He galloped his way into the Irish tradition and into the American tradition, both white and black. The truth of the matter seems to have been that he was an Irish horse in the nineteenth century of dubious colour and of doubtful form, at least as far as the Curragh racegoers were concerned. They all put their money on the other horse, which lost by a mile, obviously appealing greatly to the ballad writer.

Stewball oder Skewball war ein bemerkenswertes Pferd. Als Schimmel wie als Rappe galoppierte es in die irische und amerikanische Überlieferung. Wahr an der Geschichte scheint zu sein, daß es sich dabei um ein amerikanisches Pferd im 19. Jahrhundert handelte, das durch unbestimmte Farbe und zweifelhafte Verfassung auffiel; zumindest sahen das die Rennplatzbesucher von Curragh so. Sie alle setzten nämlich ihr Geld auf das andere Pferd, das um eine Meile abgeschlagen verlor, was offensichtlich den Verfasser dieser Ballade schwer beeindruckte.

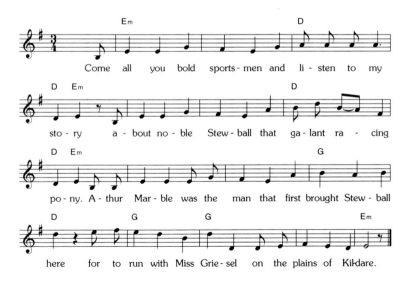

Come all you bold sportsmen and listen to my story
It's about noble Stewball that galland racing pony
Arthur Marble was the man that first brought Stewball here
For to run with Miss Griesel on the Plains of Kildare.

O the fame of his actions we've heard of before
But now he is challenged by young Mrs. Gore
For to run with Miss Griesel that handsome grey mare
For tenthousand gold guineas on the Plains of Kildare.

And the cattle they were brought out with saddle whip and bridle
And the gentlemen did shout at the sight of the gallant riders
And in viewing the cattle just as they came there
O they all laid their money on the Monaghan grey mare.

And the order it was given and away they did fly
Stewball like an arrow the grey mare passed by
And if you had've been there for to see them going round
You'd've thought to your heart their feet ne'er touched the ground.

And when at last they came to half way round the course
Stewball and his rider began to discourse
Says Stewball to the rider: Can you tell to me
How far is that grey mare this moment from me.

Says the rider to Stweball: You run in great style
You're ahead of the grey mare almost half a mile
And if you keep your running I vow and I swear
That you never will be beaten by the Monaghan grey mare.

That last winning post, Stewball passed it quite handy
Horse and rider both called for sherry wine and brandy
And they drank up a health to the noble grey mare
For she emptied their pockets on the Plains of Kildare.

Bonny Woodhall

Words: trad.
New Music: Andy Irvine

This song is Scottish in origin and though I learned it from Sam Henry's collection of songs from the North of Ireland, I have never heard it sung there. It was a big favourite with audiences but I haven't sung it for a long time now! Must relearn it one of these days.

Dieses Lied ist schottischen Ursprungs. Obwohl ich es durch Sam Henrys Liedersammlung aus dem Norden Irlands kenne, habe ich nie gehört, daß man es dort sang. Es war ein großer Renner beim Publikum, aber ich habe es lange nicht mehr gesungen. Ich werde es dieser Tage wieder einstudieren müssen!

Down by yon green bu - shes near cal - der's clear stream where me and my An - nie so of - ten have been when the hours that flew past us, right hap - py were we. It was lit - tle she thought that a sol - dier I'd be.

Down by yon green bushes near Calder's clear stream
Where me and my Annie so often have been
When the hours that flew past us, right happy were we
It was little she thought that a soldier I'd be.

But it's farewell to Annie and I must away
For the King he needs soldiers and I must obey
But if providence prove kind love until I return
I will wed with my Annie near Calder's clear burn.

On the fourteenth of August our regiment was lost
And a ball from the enemy our lines came across
O it struck me in the temple and the blod trickled down
I reeled and I staggered and I fell to the ground.

Come here says our captain come here with good speed
For I fear by this bullet young Dinsmore lies dead
Two men with a stretcher did quickly prepare
And they carried me away to a hospital there.

Cold water and brandy they pored out so free
They turned me all over my wounds for to see
But if I had my Annie to bind up my wounds
One kiss from her sweet lips would soon deaden the stoun.

And it's when I am weary and think on lang syne
When I was a miner and wrought in the mine
O the tears they do trickle and down they do fall
Like the roses that bloom around Bonny Woodhall.

Martinmas Time

Words & Music: trad., arr. Andy Irvine

Learned from Anne Briggs, who had it from the late and scorely missed A.L. Lloyd. The story of a girl dressing herself in men's clothes and fooling entire armies and navies is as old as the hills.

Ich habe dieses Lied von Anne Briggs gelernt, die es von dem verstorbenen, schmerzlich vermißten A.L. Lloyd kannte. Die Geschichte eines Mädchens, das in Männerkleidung ganze Armeen und Flotten zum Narren hält, ist so alt wie die Welt.

It fell out upon one Martinmas time
When snow lay on the border
There came a troop of soldiers here
To take up their winter quarters.

Chorus:

With me right fol adle idle e-dee-o
With me right fol adle edle eyrie.

And they rode east and they rode west
And they rode o'er the border
And there they met with a nice little girl
And she was a farmer's daughter.

And they made her swear a solemn oatch
With salt tear in her eye-o
That she would come to the quarter gates
When no one did her spy-o.

And she's gone to the tailor's shop
And dresses in soldiers clothes-o
Two long pistols down by her side
And a nice little boy was she-o.

And she's gone to the barber's shop
To the barber's shop went soon-o
Made them cut her long yellow hair
As short as any dragoon-o.

And she's gone to the quarter gates
And loundly she does call-o
There comes a troup of soldiers here
And we must have lodgings all-o.

And the Quartermaster he comes down
And gives her half a crown-o
Go find your lodgings in the town
For here there is no room-o.

But she's moved nearer to the gates
And louder she does call-o
Room, room you gentlemen
We must have lodgings all-o.

O the Quartermaster he comes down
And he gives her eighteen pence-o
Go find your lodgings in the town
For tonight there comes a wench-o.

O she took a whistle from her side
And she blew it loud and shrill-o
You're all very free with your eighteen pence
But you're not for a girl at all-o.

And she took the garters from her knees
And the ribbons from her hair-o
She's tied them around the quarter gates
As a token she's been there-o.

And when they found that it was her
They tried to have her taken
But she's clapped her spurs to her horses side
And she's galloped home a maiden.

Autumn Gold

Words & Music: Andy Irvine

Written in Ljubljana in 1968, while sitting in a sunny park, stood up on a date. Waiting, as ever, for Vida. See also „Rainy Sundays" for further material on the same subject. If I could have all the hours I spent waiting for Vida returned to me, I would take a month's holiday with it!

Geschrieben 1968 in Ljubljana, während ich in einem sonnigen Park saß und versetzt wurde. Gewartet habe ich, wie immer, auf Vida. Zur weiteren Veranschaulichung des selben Themas siehe auch „Rainy Sundays". Wenn ich all die Stunden, die ich auf Vida gewartet habe, zurück erstattet bekäme, könnte ich damit über einen Monat frei nehmen.

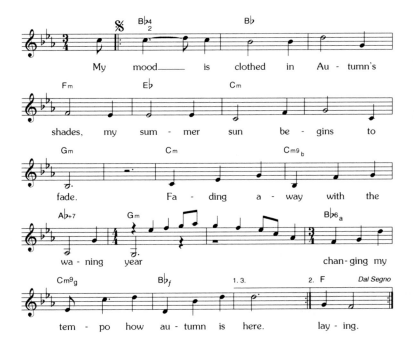

My mood is clothed in Au - tumn's shades, my sum - mer sun be - gins to fade. Fa - ding a - way with the wa - ning year chan- ging my tem - po how au - tumn is here. lay - ing.

My mood is clothed in Autumn's shades
My summer begins to fade
Fading away with the waning year
Changing my tempo now Autumn is here.

Time to leave this town with you in my mind
The dead leaves are burning
The year is declaying
Winter returning, no use in delaying.

One week ago we walked by here
I never dreamed life's death was so near
We laughed and played the summer through
The sun is going and I must go too.

Autumn Gold then Winter Snow
There's some goes south but it's north I must go
Leaving this town and the friends that I know
It's late in the year there'll be ice and snow.

When the sun returns I'll come back too
I'll write a song and I'll sing it for you.

The Rambling Siúler

New Words: Andy Irvine
Music: trad., arr. Andy Irvine

If songs about girls dressing up as men are commonplace, songs about Gentlemen dressing as beggars occur quite frequently also. Here the Colonel seems to have put on quite a good performance - despite wearing his military uniform underneath his beggars garb.

Wenn Lieder über Mädchen, die sich als Männer verkleiden, ein Allgemeinplatz sind, so sind es Lieder über Edelleute, die sich als Bettler kleiden, nicht minder. Hier scheint der Oberst eine ganz gute Vorstellung gegeben zu haben, obwohl er seine Militäruniform unter den Lumpen des Bettlers trug.

On the high-land lads are come to town and lan-ded in head-quar-ters the colo-nel fell for a pret-ty lit-le girl a far-mer's on-ly daugh-ter the gene-ral bet five hun-dred pounds the colo-nel woul-dn't dress up in a beg-gar's gown and she'll tra-vel the world go round and round will she go with the ram-bling siú-ler.

31

The highland lads are come to town
And landed in headquarters
The Colonel fell for a pretty little girl
A farmer's only daughter
The General bet five thousand pounds
The Colonel would'nt dress up in a beggar's gown
And she'll travel the world go round and round
Will she go with the rambling siúler.

The Colonel startet out next day
Dressed in a beggar's clothing
It wasn't long till he found his way
To the farmer's lowly dwelling
O farmer shelter me for the night
I'll sleep in your barn until daylight
Take pity on a beggar's awful plight
God help all rambling siúlers.

The farmer says the night is wet
You can come to the kitchen fire
The Colonel says to the serving maid
It's you I do admire
Will you leave them all and come with me
Leave them all a grá mo chroi
What as lusty beggar you would be
Away with the rambling siúler.

The farmer and his servants all
They fell into loud laughter
When who came tripping won the stairs
But the farmer's only daughter
She'd two eyes like the morning skies
Soon as the beggar he did her spy
She fairly caught his rambling eye
She'll be mine says the rambling siúler.

The farmer and his servants all
They went out to the byre
He put his arm around her waist
As they sat by the kitchen fire
He put his hand upon her knee
Unto her gave kisses three
Says she how dare you make so free
And it's you but a rambling siúler.

When supper it was over-o
They made his bed in the barn
Between two sacks and a winnow cloth
For fear that he'd do harm
But at twelve o'clock that very night
She came to the barn she was dressed in white
The beggar rose in great delight
She's mine says the rambling siúler.

And he threw off his beggar's clothes
He threw them against the wall-o
He stood the bravest gentleman
That was almost them all-o
Will you look at my locks of golden hair
Under the sooty old hat I wear
I'm a colones bold I do declare
And it's not but a rambling siúler.

And I wouldn't for one hundred pounds
That you and I would be found here
Will you travel around the whole night long
And go with the rambling siúler
Oh it's off to the General's house they've gone
Great is the wager he has won
Salute them both with the fife and the drum
She's away with the rambling siúler.

You Rambling Boys Of Pleasure

Words & Music: trad., arr. Andy Irvine

This is probably my favourite song of all time. Learned from the singing of two of my heroes, Len Graham and the late Joe Holmes. Whatever negative feelings some people may have about folksongs, when it comes to songs of unrequited love, the anonymous folk composer was certainly in his element and in this song, at the peak of his poetic genius.

Dies ist wohl schon immer mein Lieblingslied gewesen. Gelernt habe ich es aus dem Repertoire zweier meiner Idole, von Len Graham und dem verstorbenen Joe Holmes. Welch negative Gefühle auch immer manche Leute Volksliedern entgegen bringen mögen, handelt es sich um Lieder über unerwiderte Liebe, so war der anonyme Volkskomponist sicherlich in seinem Element und bei diesem Lied auf dem absoluten Gipfel seiner dichterischen Eingebung.

of - ten - times she does me slight. My mind is ne - ver ea - sy ex - cept when my true love is in my sight.

You rambling boys of pleasure
Give ear unto these lines I write
I own I am a rover
In rambling I take great delight
I cast my mind on a handsome girl
And oftentimes she does me slight
My mind is never easy
Except when my true love is in my sight.

Down by yon flowery gardens
Where me and my true love do meet
I took her in my arms
And unto her gave kisses sweet
She bade me take love easy
Just as the leaves fall from the tree
But I being young and foolish
With my own true love I did not agree.

And the second time I met my love
I thought that her heart was surely mine
But as the season changes
My darling girl has changed her mind
Gold is the root of evil
Although its bears a glistening hue

Causes many's the lad and the lass to part
Though their hearts like mine be e'er so true.
And I should be whish I was in Belfast town
And my true love along with me
And money in my pocket
To keep us in good company
Liquor to be plenty
A flowing glass on every side
Hard fortune would ne'er daunt me
For I am young and the world is wide.

Smeceno Horo

Music: trad., arr. Andy Irvine

On my travels in Eastern Europe, many years ago, I bought an Album of
Bulgarian music in Sofia. I had it in my rucksack for nine months after that
before I got a chance to play it. It was in bits when I got it home, but this tune
was on it without a scratch.

Auf meinen Reisen durch Osteuropa kaufte ich vor vielen Jahren in Sofia eine
Schallplatte mit bulgarischer Musik. Danach trug ich sie neun Monate mit mir
herum, bevor sich eine Möglichkeit ergab, sie abzuspielen. Sie war in Stücke
zersprungen, als ich zu Hause ankam, doch diese Melodie hatte ohne einen
Kratzer überlebt.

37

Roger O'Hehir

New Words & Music: Andy Irvine

Roger seems to have been quite famous as a highwayman in the early nineteenth century. However his crimes, as listed here, are pretty petty and he certainly doesn't seem to have been very good at it. Learned from Sam Henry's collection „Songs of the People". A collection that has been like a bible to me.

Roger war, wie es scheint, ein recht berühmter Wegelagerer im frühen 19. Jahrhundert, obwohl seine Verbrechen, wie sie hier beschrieben werden, recht armselig sind und er sicherlich keine gute Figur dabei abgegeben haben dürfte. Kennengelernt habe ich dieses Lied durch Sam Henrys Sammlung „Songs of the People". Für mich war diese Sammlung wie eine Bibel.

At the Eight Mile Bridge in the Count - ty Down I had hon - est pa - rents of fame and re - nown. O had I been o - be - dient and kept the com - mand I ne - ver would have bro - ken the laws of the land. Right fol ol the day.

At the Eight Mile Bridge in the County Down
I had honest parents of fame and renown
O had I been obedient and kept the command
I never would have broken the laws of the land.

Chorus

Right fol ol the day.

My parents endeavoured to give me honest bread
They bound me apprentice onto the linen trade
All to an honest weaver that lived hard by
My mind being for rambling it would not comply.

One beautiful creature Jane Sharkey by name
I gained her affection and I was to blame
I own I enticed her and we ran away
My troubles began from the very same day.

That beautiful creature I soon left forlorn
For fear of her parents I stepped up to Mourne
But her cruel father pursued my with spite
He made me his prisoner the very same night.

And the guards they pursued me the very next day
The guards I beguiled and I soon got away
I went down to the shore where a vessel it did lay
I set my foot on shipboard and to England sailed away.

And it's when that I landed in sweet Holyhead
I had no honest means for to earn my bread
And I was loathe to beg but alas I did worse
To make myself money I stole a grey horse.

And it's when that I landed once more on Irish ground
I soon began my tricks again near fair Newry town
For I stole a hat from one Thomas Wright
He made me his prisoner the very same night.

And it's off to Newry guardhouse once more I was sent
To hang me next morning it was their intent
When I heard of this well it put me in a fright
I knocked down the turnkey and excaped in the same night.

And the guards they pursued my again the same way
The guards I beguiled and once more I got away
Says one into the other he'll travel no more
The very same night Newry Lough I swam o'er.

And I rested myself for a day or two more
I went to rob a Bleachgreen where I never was before
But they were strong with guards in the Bleachgreen within
Surrounded was poor Roger and taken was again.

Now Roger was taken but often did get free
It's come now to his turn for to march to the tree
And all his foolish actions he there did declare
And that put an end to bold Roger O'Hehir.

Kellswater

New Words & Music: Andy Irvine

Another song from the North of Ireland. If a father did not care for the boy his daughter had set her heart on (usually for class reasons) he would either have him murdered or sent to America.

Ein weiteres Lied aus dem Norden Irlands. Wenn ein Vater den jungen Mann, an den seine Tochter ihr Herz verloren hatte, nicht akzeptierte (üblicherweise aus Standesgründen), so ließ er ihn entweder ermorden oder nach Amerika fortbringen.

Here's a health to you___ Bon - ny Kells - wa - ter,

where you get all the plea - sures___ of___ life,

where you get all the___ fish - ing and___ fow - ling

and a bon - ny wee___ lass___ for your wife.

O it's down where yon___ wa - ters run___ mud - dy.

I'm a - fraid they will ne - ver___ run___ clear and it's

when I be - gin for to___ stu - dy my___

mind___ is on___ them___ that's not here.

Here's a health to you Bonny Kellswater
Where you get all the pleasures of life
Where you get all the fishing and fowling
And a bonny wee lass for your wife
O it's down where yon waters run muddy
I'm afraid they will never run clear
And it's when I begin for to study
My mind is on them that's not here.

For it's this one and that one may court him
But if anyone gets him but me
It's early and late I will curse them
That parted lovely Willie from me
O father he calls on his daughter
Two choices I'll give unto thee
Would you rather see Willie's ship a-sailing
Or see him hung like a dog from yon tree.

O father dear father I love him
I can no longer hide it from thee
Through an acre of fire I would travel
Along with lovely Willie to be
But it's woe to the heart that confines me
And keeps me from my hearts delight
Strong walls and cold irons they bind me
And a stone for my pillow at night.

O yonders a ship on the ocean
And she does not know which way to steer
From the east to the west she's a-blowing
She reminds me on the charms of my dear
O it's yonder my Willie he will be coming
He said he'd be there in spring
And down by yon green shades I'll meet him
And among yon wild roses we'll sing.

For a gold ring he placed on my finger
Saying love bear this in your mind
If ever I sail from old Ireland
You'll mind I'll not leave you behind
Farewell to you bonny Kellswater
Where you'll get all the pleasures of life
Where you'll get all the fishing and fowling
And a bonny wee lass your wife.

Johnny Of Brady's Lea

Words: trad.
Music: Andy Irvine

This is a version of an old classic ballad usually called „Johnny O'Breadislee".
It has the drama of Greek Tragedy, Johnny's fate being sealed from the outset.

Dies ist eine Version einer klassischen Ballade, die meistens „Johnny
O'Breadislee" genannt wird. Wie in der griechischen Tragödie ist Johnnys
Schicksal hier von vornherein besiegelt.

Johnny arose on a May morning
Called for water to wash his hands
Says bring to me two grey dogs
That lay bound in Iron bands.

When Johnny's mother she heard of this
She wrung her hands full sore
Says Johnny for you vension
To the greenwoods do not go.

For there are seven foresters in Esselmont
And this you know full well
For one small drop of your hearts blood
The would ride through the gates of Hell.

O there's many men are my friend mother
Though many more are my foe
And betide me well or betide me ill
A-hunting I will go.

So Johnny has taken his good bend bow
And his arrows one by one
And he's away to Monymusk
To bring the dun deer down.

Johnny shot and the dun deer leaped
And he's wounded her in the side
And between the waters and the woods
The two dogs laid her pride.

And they ate so much of the vension
And they drank so much of the blood
That Johnny and his two grey dogs
Fell asleep as if they had been dead.

And by there came a silly old man
And an ill death may he dee
And he's away to Esselmont
To tell on young Johnny.

As I came in by Monymusk
And down among yon scrogs
It was there I spied the bonniest youth
Lying sleeping between two dogs.

And the buttons that were on his coat
The were of the gold so good
And the two grey dogs that he lay between
Their mouths were dyed with blood.

Then up and spoke the first forester
He was headsman over them all
Can this be Johnny of Brady's lea
Unto him we will draw.

And the very first shot that the foresters fired
Well it wounded him in the thigh
And the very next shot that the foresters fired
His hearts blood blended his eye.

Then up woke Johnny from out of his sleep
And an angry man was he
He says the wildest wolf in all this wood
Would not have done so by me.

And he's leaned his back against and oak
And his foot against a stone
And he has fired on the seven foresters
And he's killed them all but one.

And he's broken seven of this mans ribs
His arm and his collar bone
And he has set him unto his horse
To bring the tidings home.

Now Johhny's good bend bow is broke
And his two grey dogs are slain
And his body lies in Monymusk
And his hunting days are done.

Thousands Are Sailing

New Words & Music: Andy Irvine

I first heard this song sung by another hero of mine, Eddie Butcher from Magilligan, County Derry. It has also been recorded by Cathal McConnell and Robin Morton. It is a typical broadside ballad - that is, it was probably sold at fairs and public holidays printed on a sheet of paper and sung by the seller. A finely descriptive song.

Zuerst hörte ich dieses Lied von einem meiner anderen Idole, von Eddie Butcher aus Magilligan, County Derry. Es wurde auch von Cathal McConnel und Robin Morton aufgenommen. Es ist eine typische Flugblatt-Ballade, welche auf einem Papierbogen gedruckt, auf Jahrmärkten verkauft und dabei vom Verkäufer gesungen wurde. Ein ausgesprochen anschauliches Lied.

You brave Irish heroes wherever you be
I pray stand a moment and listen to me
Your sons and fair daughters are now going away
And thousands are sailing to Amerikay.

So good luck to those people and safe they may land
They are leaving their country for a far distant strand
They are leaving old Ireland no longer can stay
And thousands are sailing to Amerikay.

The night before leaving they are bidding goodbye
And its early next morning their heart gives a sigh
They do kiss their mothers and then they will say
Farewell dear old father we must go away.

Their friends and relations and neighbours also
When the trunks are all packed up and ready to go
The tears from their eyes they fall down like the rain
And the horses are pracing going off for the train.

When they do reach the station you will hear their last cry
With handkerchiefs waving and bidding goodbye
Their hearts will be breaking on leaving the shore
Farewell dear old Ireland will we ne'er see you more?

O I pity the mother that rears up the child
And likewise the father who labours and toils
To try to support them he'll work night and day
And when they are reared up they will go away.

So good luck to those people and safe they may land
They are leaving their country for a far distant strand
They are leaving old Ireland no longer can stay
And thousands are sailing to Amerikay.

48

Napoleon Bonaparte

Words & Music: trad., arr. Andy Irvine

Learned from Dolores Keane and John Faulkner. Many's the girl in Ireland would have waited in vain for her loved one to return from the European battlefields.

Gelernt von Dolores Keane und John Faulkner. So manches Mädchen in Irland hat vergeblich darauf gewartet, daß ihr Liebster von den europäischen Schlachtfeldern heimkehrte.

O Na - po - le - on Bo - na - parte you're the cause of my woe since my bon - ny light horse - man to the wars he did go. Bro - ken hear - ted I'll wan - der, bro - ken hear - ted I'll re - main since my bon - ny light horse - man in the wars he was slain.

O Napoleon Bonaparte you're the cause of my woe
Since my bonny light Horseman to the wars he did go
Broken hearted I'll wander broken hearted I'll remain
Since my bonny light horseman in the wars he was slain.

When Boney commanded his armies to stand
And proudly waved his banners all gaily and grand
He levelled his cannon right over the plain
And my bonny light horseman in the battle was slain.

O Napoleon Bonaparte you're the cause of my woe
Since my bonny light Horseman to the wars he did go
Broken hearted I'll wander broken hearted I'll remain
Since my bonny light horseman in the wars he was slain.

And if I was some small bird and had wings and could fly
I would fly o'er the salt sea where my true love does lie
Three years and six months now since he left this bright shore
O my bonny light horseman will I ne'er see you more?

O Napoleon Bonaparte you're the cause of my woe
Since my bonny light Horseman to the wars he did go
Broken hearted I'll wander broken hearted I'll remain
Since my bonny light horseman in the wars he was slain.

And the dove she laments for her mate as she flies
O where tell me where is my true love she sighs
O where in this wide world is there one to compare
With my bonny light horseman who was killed in the war.

O Napoleon Bonaparte you're the cause of my woe
Since my bonny light Horseman to the wars he did go
Broken hearted I'll wander broken hearted I'll remain
Since my bonny light horseman in the wars he was slain.

General Monroe

Words & Music: trad., arr. Andy Irvine

Henry Monroe was chosen to lead insurgents of County Down in the 1798 rebellion. He was victorious at Saintfield but defeated at Ballynahinch on 13th of June. He hid in a farm but was betrayed and hanged in front of his own house, three days later. This song was quite popular during the „Ballad Boom" in Ireland around 1967.

Henry Monroe war gewählter Anführer der Rebellen aus dem County Down beim Aufstand von 1798. Siegreich war er bei Saintfield, doch bei Ballynahinch wurde er am 13. Juni geschlagen. Er versteckte sich auf einem Bauernhof, wurde jedoch verraten und drei Tage später vor seinem eigenen Haus aufgehängt. Dieses Lied war während des „Balladen Booms" um 1967 in Irland sehr beliebt.

My name is George Camp - bell my age is six - teen. I joined the U - ni - ted men to fight for the green and ma - ny's the bat - tle I did un - der go when com - mand - ed by that he - ro bold Ge - ne - ral Mon - roe.

My name is George Campbell my age is sixteen
I joined the United men to fight for the green
And many's the battle I did undergo
When commanded by that hero bold General Monroe.

Were you at the battle of Ballynahinch?
When the people opressed rose up in defence
And Monroe took the mountains and his men took the field
And they fought for three hours and never did yield.

Monroe being weary and in need of some sleep
He gave a woman ten guineas his secret to keep
But when she got the money the devil tempted her so
That she sent for the army and surrendered Monroe.

Well the army they came and surrounded them all
He thought to escape but he could not all
And they marched him to Lisburn without more delay
And they hung our bold hero the very same day.

Were you at the farm when the cavalry came there
How the horses did caper and prance in the rear
And the traitor being with them as you all know
It was out of a haystack they hauled poor Monroe.

In came Monroe's sister she was well dressed in green
She'd a sword by her side that was long sharp and keen
Three cheers she did give and away she did go
Saying I'll have revenge for my brother Monroe.

Monroe being taken and led to the tree
He says farewell to my comrades whereever they may be
There's one thing that grieves me and thats parting them so
So farewell to that hero brave General Monroe.

Farewell To Old Ireland

Words & Music: trad., arr. Andy Irvine

Related to „The Greenfields of Canada" and to numerous other songs depicting the emigration of the Irish to the United States in the 1850's and 1860's. Virtually all of which are worth singing.

Verwandt mit „The Greenfields of Canada" und zahlreichen anderen Liedern, welche die Geschichte der irischen Auswanderung in die Vereinigten Staaten während der 50er und 60er Jahre des neunzehnten Jahrhunderts erzählen. Alle sind es eigentlich wert, gesungen zu werden.

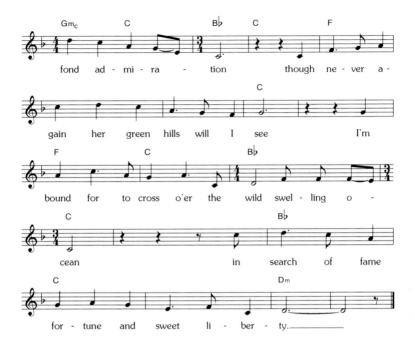

fond ad - mi - ra - tion though ne - ver a -
gain her green hills will I see I'm
bound for to cross o'er the wild swel - ling o -
cean in search of fame
for - tune and sweet li - ber - ty.

Farewell to old Ireland the land of my childhood
That now and foreever I bound for to leave
Farewell to the shores where the shamrock is growing
It's the bright spot of beauty and the home of the brave
I will think on her valleys with fond admiration
Though never again her green hills will I see
I'm bound for to cross o'er the wild swelling ocean
In search of fame fortune and sweet liberty.

It's hard to be forced from the lands that we live in
Our houses and farms we're obliged for to sell
And to wander alone among Indians and strangers
To seek home sweet spot where our children my dwell
O I have a wee lassie I fain would take with me
Her dwelling at present lies in County Down
It would break my poor heart to leave her behind me
We'll both roam together this wide world around.

So it's come along Bessie my own blue lassie
Bid farewell to your mother and then come with me
And I'll make all endeavour my love maintain you
Till we reach the green fields of Amerikay
So it's lift up your glasses you lads and gay lassies
There's gold for the winning and lots of it too
Here's health to the part that has courage to venture
Bad luck to the lad or the lass that would rue.

Our ship at the present lies in Derry harbour
To bear us away o'er the wild swelling sea
May heaven be her pilot and grant us fond breezes
Till we reach the green fields of Amerikay
O come to the land where we will be happy
Don't be afraid of the storm or the sea
And it's when we get over we will surely discover
That place in the land of sweet liberty.

There's brandy in Quebec at ten cents a quart, me boys
The ale in New Brunswick's a penny a glass
There's wine in that sweet town they call Montreal, boys
At Inn after Inn we will drink as we pass
And we'll call for a bumper of ale, wine and brandy
And we'll drink to the health of those far far away
Our hearts will all warm at the thoughts of old Ireland
When we're in the green fields of Amerikay.

Edward Connors

Words & Music: trad., arr. Andy Irvine

I learned this highly descriptive ballad from Eddie Butcher who had a final verse where Edward Connors sailed home again. A happy ending but a slightly implausible one.

Ich lernte diese äußerst stimmungsvolle Ballade von Eddie Butcher, bei dem Edward Connors in der letzten Strophe wieder nach Hause segelte. Ein glückliches Ende zwar, doch wenig einleuchtend.

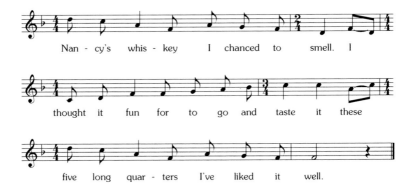

Nan - cy's whis - key I chanced to smell. I

thought it fun for to go and taste it these

five long quar - ters I've liked it well.

These five long quarters I have been weaving
And for my weaving I was paid down
I bought a shirt in the foremost fashion
All for to walk up thro' Longford town
Where Nancy's whiskey I chanced to smell
I thought it fun for to go and taste it
These five long quarters I've liked it well.

I entered into a little alehouse
Begged Nancy's pardon for making free
And Nancy met me at every corner
You're hearty welcome young man says she
We both sat down at a little table
We looked at each other a little while
We both sat down at a little table
And Nancy's whiskey did me beguile.

I found meself then in a little parlor
I found meself then in a liitle bed
I tried to rise but I was not able
For Nancy's whiskey it held down me head
When I arose, aye, the following morning
I asked the reckoning I had to pay
It's fifeteen shillings for ale and porter
Come pay it quickly now and get away.
I put the money out on the table

Saying I'll leave this money down with the rest
And I'll drink a health to very young man
And the wee lassie that I loved best
And I'll go home I'll begin me weaving
I'll steer my shuttle another while
And if I live for another reason
It's Nancy's whiskey will not me beguile.

Farewell To Ballymoney

Words & Music: trad., arr. Andy Irvine

Another song of unrequited love, which was definitely a forte of the folk composer. This song causes the unhappy lover to leave his native shore.

Ein weiteres Lied über unerwiderte Liebe, zweillos eine Stärke des Volkskomponisten. In diesem nun muß der unglücklich Liebende seine heimatlichen Gefilde verlassen.

val - ley where stands my heart's de - light and it's with you love-ly Mol - ly I'll spend till broad day - light.

O courting is a pleasure between my love and I
I'll go down to yon low valley where she'll meet me by and by
I'll go down to yon low valley where stands my hearts delight
And it's with you lovely Molly I will spend till broad daylight.

Coming home from Church last Sunday my love she passed me by
I could tell her mind was changing by the roving of her eye
I could tell her mind was changing to man of high degree
O Molly dearest Molly your love has wounded me.

I went up to my true love with a bottle in my hand
Saying drink of this dear Molly our courtship ne'er will stand
Saying drink of this dear Molly let the bottle and glass go free
For ten guineas lies in wagers that married we ne'er will be.

O there's some do court in earnest while others court in fun
But I can court the old sweetheart and bring the new one on
I can tell her loving stories to keep her mind at ease
But as soon as she has her back turned on me I am courting
        whoe'er I please.

Never court a sweetheart with a dark rolling eye
Kiss her and embrace her but don't tell her the reason why
O kiss her and embrace till you get her heart to yield
For a faint hearted soldier never won the battlefield.

Like the town of Ballymoney and the County Antrim too
Likewise my darling Molly I bid you a now adieu
America lies far away it's land I will go see
May all bad luck attend the lad that parted my love and me.

Romanian Song (Blood And Gold)

Words: Jane Cassidy
Music: Andy Irvine

I heard a great Macedonian tune when I was there many years ago but I didn't understand the words. Some time later I came across a Romanian song collected by Béla Bartok, himself a Hungarian. Jane Cassidy largely forged the verses of the song from the translation and so we have here a Pan-European effort.

Vor vielen Jahren hörte ich in Madzedonien ein großartiges Lied, verstand jedoch den Text nicht. Einige Zeit später stieß ich auf ein rumänisches Lied, das Béla Bartok aufgezeichnet hatte, der selbst ein Ungar war. Jane Cassidy gestaltete diesen Text nach einer Übersetzung und so haben wir hier das Ergebnis einer paneuropäischen Zusammenarbeit.

weep no more you are gone_____

_____ to kill_____ and die.

O rides a captain and threehundred soldier lads
Out of the morning mist thro' the silent snow
Whistling gaily rides the captain at their head
Behind him soldier boys sadly weeping go.

O lads of mine weep no more
You are gone to kill and die.

For when you took my gold and swore to follow me
You sold away your lives and your liberty
No more you'll till the soil, no more you'll work the land
No more to the dance you'll go and take the girls by the hand.

O mother weep for your son
He is gone to kill and die.

You'll weep, you'll die by the keen edge of the sword
All alone by the muddy Danube shore
He gave the order for the drummer to beat their drums
That mothers all might know the life a soldier leads.

O mothers weep for your sons
They are gone to kill an die.

Unfurl your ragged banners and raise your pale young face
You'll all go in the fire there'll be no hiding place
O mother hear that drumbeat in the village square
O mother that drums for me to go for a soldier there.

Mothers, sisters, wives, weep for us
Marked as Cain we lie alone.

King Bore And The Sandman

Words & Music: Andy Irvine

Dedicated to the man in the public house we are always trying to avoid ... I wrote this song in Romania on my travels back in 1968.

Dem Mann in der Kneipe gewidmet, die wir ja immer zu meiden suchen ... Ich schrieb dieses Lied auf meinen Reisen 1968 in Rumänien.

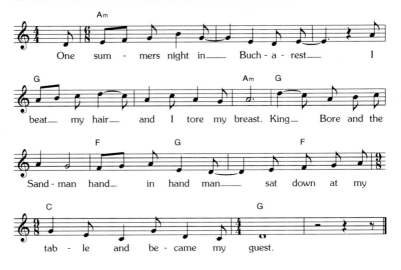

One summers night in Bucharest
I bear my hair and I tore my breast
King Bore and the Sandman
Hand in hand man
Sat down at my table and became my guest.

I knew by the look in his boring eyes
I knew by the witless old grey head so wise
When he took out an oilcan
And oiled his jaws man
I knew I was in for no great surprise.

And lo and behold his mouth opened wide
And his rusty old tongue which had long lain inside
Issued forth with a torrent
Of words so abhorrent
I had never a chance of stemming the tide.

My eyes were glazed and my neck was sore
From nodding my head for three hours or more
When King Bore with a roar
Tore my heart to the core
For he saw my eyes travel across the room to the door.

„I'm not boring you, I hope" said he
And instantly launched into soliloquy
Of his youthful frolics such a load of old rubbish
As I ever have heard you can take it from me.

But to my amazement, relief and surprise
The Sandman yawned and up he did rise
And from out of his handbag
Produced a sandbag
And a handful he threw in my red rimmed eyes.

The very last words I heard the old King say
„When I was in Amerikay ..."
My departing mind
Left him far behind
And King Bore and the Sandman they both faded away.

Rainy Sundays

Words & Music: Andy Irvine

Ever the one to follow the heart and not the head, I pursued a one sided romance in Lubljana a long time ago. It came to nothing but remained with me a long time afterwards ...

Immer bereit, dem Herzen und nicht dem Verstand zu folgen, verrannte ich mich vor langer Zeit in Lubljana in eine einseitige Romanze. Es wurde nichts daraus, doch sie ließ mich lange nichts mehr los ...

Rai - ny Sun - days win - dy dreams, no - thing appears to be as sim - ple as it seems.

Down in Lju - bl - ja - ma, they've
ne - ver seen such a mot - ley crew.

Some in search of Nir - va - na and some of us with
no - thing else to do. On - ly stopped for a
mo - ment to shel - ter from the rain was - n't till five months
la - ter that I was trav - elling a - gain, if you're
hea - ding down towards the East stay on the road my

Rainy Sundays, windy dreams
Nothing appears to be as simple as it seems.

Down in Ljubljana, they've never seen such a motley crew
Some search of Nirvana and some of us with nothing else to do
Only stopped for a moment to shelter from the rain
It wasn't till five months later, that I was travelling again
If you're heading down towards the East
Stay on the road my friend
Don't break your heart for Vida
In a Slovenian dead end.

Rainy sundays, windy dreams
Clouding memories, fading scenes.

In a Supermarket storeroom, it's dirty but it's where we all doss down
It's underneath the cold ground, no shaft of light has ever shown us round
Wake up in the morning (or is it the afternoon?)
And its rumoured every evening
Police are going to get us soon
But they never do and anyway, I'd die a hero's death
For when I'm in her company, the world holds it's breath.

Rainy Sundays, sodden feet flap along on the flags
Zany, somedays, me and the boys we fall around at the gags
When I'm waiting for Vida
Get drunk as a rule
When I finally see her
Does she think I'm a fool?
For she wears an air of mystery
It suits her well my heart upon my sleeve
Hope it doesn't show.

But it's only make believe
Visions in a waking dream
Like dust that dances in a hazy sunbeam
Sometimes at night
Wake with a start
To see your smile
Fade in the dark.

Rainy Sundays, windy dreams
Can't seem to rid myself of these nostalgic scenes.

At the station waiting, as sullen clouds scud across the sky
Humiliating, the birds on the grey wind seem to cry
All my companions are seated on the train
Going to spend the day at sea but she's let me down again
And as the train rolls down the line
I roll back into town
To sear old haunts
For she who taunts
Her lonely hand-me-down.

One Sunday at the skating, told her I was tired of playing pretend
Incapacitating, these windy dreams that are my childhood friend

Until you play them wrong
For she cried when I was leaving
And now she's long gone
But the moments flown and so's the luck
As lucky moments may
And a windy dream can come unstuck
On any Rainy Sunday.

Standing on the Sava's banks
That random moment's trapped in time
The ghost of you still stalks across my mind
A smiling girl
Turns her back
Walks away
Fades to black.

Willy O'Winsbury

Words & Music: trad., arr. Andy Irvine

The ultimate happy-ending, romantic ballad. I learned this from Professor Child's definitive collection. Looking up the tune in the back of the book, I inadvertently, picked the wrong one, which by chance fitted the song perfectly. I really enjoyed singing this song in 2005 with „Planxty" on some of the gigs we did on our reunion tour.

Die romantische Ballade mit glücklichem Ausgang schlechthin. Ich lernte dieses Lied durch Professor Childs Standardwerk kennen. Als ich die Melodie am Ende des Buches nachschlagen wollte, erwischte ich versehentlich eine falsche, die aber zufällig hervorragend zum Text paßte. Ich genoß es ausgesprochen, dieses Lied mit „Planxty" bei einigen Gigs auf unserer Wiedervereinigungstournee 2005 zu singen.

The king has been a poor prisoner
A prisoner long in Spain
And Willy o' the Winsbury
Has lain long with his daughter at home.

What troubles you my daughter dear
You look so pale and wan
O have you had any sore sickness
Or yet been sleeping with a man.

I have not had any sore sickness
Nor yet been sleeping with a man
It is for you my father dear
For biding long in Spain.

Cast off, cast off your berry brown gown
Stand naked upon a stone
That I may ken you by your shape
Whether you be a maiden or none.

So she's cast off her berry brown gown
Stood naked upon a stone

Her haunches were round and her apron was short
Her cheeks they were pale and wan.

O is he a Lord or a Duke or a Knight
Or a man of birth or fame
Or is he one of my servingmen
That's lately come out of Spain?

He is not a Lord nor a Duke nor a Knight
Nor a man of birth or fame
But he is Willy O'Winsbury
Could bide nae langer my laim.

The King has sent for his merry men all
His merry men thirty and three
Says bring me Willy O'Winsbury
For hanged he shall be.

But when he came the King before
He was clad in the red silk
His hair was like the strands of gold
His cheeks were as white as milk.

It is no wonder says the King
My daughter's love you did win
Had I been a woman as I am a man
My bedfellow you would have been.

And will you marry my daughter Janet
By the truth of your right hand
And will you marry my daughter Janet
And be a Lord of the land?

Aye, I will marry your daughter Janet
By the truth of my right hand
And I will marry your daughter Janet
But I won't be a Lord of the land.

He's mounted her on a milk-white steed
Himself on a dapple grey
And he's made her lady of as much land
And she could ride in a long summers day.

Creggan White Hare

New Words & Music: Andy Irvine

A fairly modern, local ballad. I'm sure people of the area would even remember who wrote it. I learned it from an old BBC disc, recorded in 1952 by Sean O'Boyle and Peter Kennedy. The singer was Vincent Donnelly from Castle Caulfield, County Tyrone.

Eine recht moderne Ballade mit Lokalkolorit. Ich bin davon überzeugt, daß sich Leute aus der Gegend sogar noch daran erinnern können, wer sie geschrieben hat. Ich lernte sie durch eine alte BBC-Schallplatte kennen, die Sean O'Boyle und Peter Kennedy 1952 aufgenommen haben. Sänger war Vincent Donnelly aus Castle Caulfield, County Tyrone.

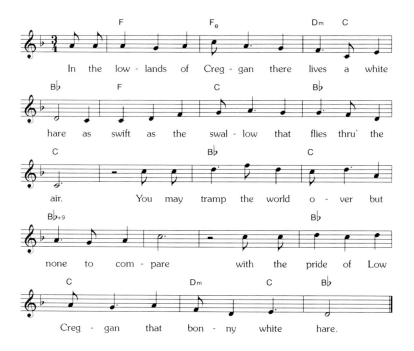

In the low-lands of Creg-gan there lives a white hare as swift as the swal-low that flies thru' the air. You may tramp the world o-ver but none to com-pare with the pride of Low Creg-gan that bon-ny white hare.

In the lowlands of Creggan there lives a white hare
As swift as the swallow that flies through the air
You may tramp the world over but none to compare
With the pride of Low Creggan that bonny white hare.

Till one clear Autumn morning as you may suppose
The red golden sun o'er the green mountain rose
Barney Conway came down and he did declare
This day I'll put an end to that bonny white hare.

He searched through the lowlands and down through the glens
And among the green bushes where the white hare had ends
Till at last coming o'er the heather so bare
From behind a wild thistle out jumped the white hare.

He fired off his gun and his dog he loosed to
As swift as the wind o'er the montain they flew
But the dog he came back which made poor Barney sigh
For he knew that the white hare had bid him goodbye.

We're some jolly sportsmen down here from Pomeroy
From Cookstown, Dungannon and likewise The Moy
With our pedigree greyhounds we're travelled afar
And we've come down to Creggan in our fine motor car.

Away to the Lowlands these huntsmen did go
To seek for the white hare they looked high and low
Till at last Barney Conway on a turf bank so bare
Shouted out to the huntsmen there goes the white hare.

They called up their greyhounds from off the green lea
And Barney and the huntsmen they jumped high with glee
For there on a turf bank all gathered around
Seven dogs and nine men did that poor hare surround.

No wonder the white hare did tremble with fear
As she stood on her toes and she would raise her big ears
She stood on her toes and with one gallant spring
She leaped over the greyhounds and broke through the ring.

The chase it went on it was a beautiful view
As swift as the wind o'er the green mountain flew
But the pedigree greyhounds they didn't go far
They came back and went home in their fine motor car.

There came another man and you all know him well
His name is Pat Devlin and bonny black Nell
In search of the white hare he says I'll have fun
Here's fifty to one that black Nell will her turn.

Five turns the hare got then from bonny black Nell
The sixth one was given around John Haughey's well
Twas there we lost sight of the hare and the dog
And in five minutes later came o'er the black dog.

The chase it went on it was great for to see
The white hare and the greyhound they roamed light and free
She travelled to Eskra where she new the lands well
And bonny black Nellie she soon bid farewell.

And now to conclude and to finish it's time
I hope you'll forgive me for singing this rhyme
If there's any amongst you in Carrickmore fair
Lets drink up a health to that bonny white hare.

At Twenty-One

Words: trad./ Andy Irvine
Music: Andy Irvine

Learned from Robert Cinnamond, County Antrim. This is a real tearjerker. I suppose you could hardly blame the girl for giving her hand to the man with the money, hopefully she loved him as well as his money. It was a bit rough on the local lad though, who watched his future happiness sail away because of his impoverished circumstances.

Gelernt von Robert Cinnamond, County Antrim. Ein richtiges Rührstück. Man kann, wie ich meine, dem Mädchen, das seine Hand dem reichen Mann gab, keinen Vorwurf machen, wenn sie ihn so sehr liebte wie sein Geld. Dennoch war es ziemlich hart für den Dorfburschen, sein zukünftiges Glück entschwinden zu sehen, nur weil er in ärmlichen Verhältnissen lebte.

gree._____ T'was well i knew she would prove
true and loy - al un - to me.

At twenty-one I first begun
To court my neighbour's child
We both being young and full of fun
Bright Phoebus on us smiled
We both being young and full of fun
Right well we did agree
Twas well I knew she would prove true
And loyal into me.

At twenty-two no man could view
All the beauty that this maid posessed
Her curling hair in ringlets fair
Hung down her snow white breast
The picture of her two blue eyes
My pencil cannot tell
Her effigy no hand could draw
Nor paint her parallel.

At twenty-four I did adore
This beautiful young fair maid
When she gave her hand
To a rich young man
Alas but I was poor
They sailed away across the sea
And left me here to mourn
That bright May day she sailed away
Never more for to return.

Captain Colston

Words & Music: trad., arr Andy Irvine

Learned from an old recording of Peter O'Donnell from County Tyrone. It's hard to believe that human beings would prey upon poor people emigrating. However, enter the Captain's wife, exit the Pirate Captain. All's well that end's well.

Dieses Lied habe ich durch eine alte Aufnahme mit Peter O'Donell aus dem County Tyrone kennen gelernt. Kaum zu glauben, daß menschliche Wesen arme Leute, die emigrieren wollen, ausgeplündert haben. Wie auch immer: Kapitänsfrau taucht auf, Piratenkapitän tritt ab. Ende gut, alles gut.

You lands-men all on you I call you he - roes stout and brave____ that are in - clined to cross the sea, your home - land now to leave.____ Come join with Cap - tain Col - ston that he - ro stout and bold____ who fought his way all on the sea and ne - ver was con - trolled.

You landsmen all on you I call you heroes stout and brave
That are inclined to cross the sea, your homeland now to leave
Come join with Captain Colston that hero stout and bold
Who fought his way all on the sea and never was controlled.

O we sailed away from Liverpool the weather being fine
Bound for New York city boys, it was our chief design
We being all Irish emigrants the truth to you I'll tell
Who in distress our homes had left and to Ireland bid farewell.

On the evening of the twenty fith our captain he did cry
Clear away the decks me boys for a strange asyl I do spy
And all you Irish emigrants awake now from your sleep
For in a few more hours me boys you'll be slumbering in the deep.
For a pirate ship is coming down just from the western sea
For to rob us of our property going to Amerikay

O the pirate ship came up to us and ordered us to stand
Your gold and precious cargo this moment I demand
Your gold and precious loading resign to me this day
Fore one living soul you'll never bring into Amerikay.

Then up and spoke our captain with voice both loud and bold
Saying we will slumber in the deep before we'll be controlled
Before that we'll surrender our property to thee
We'll fight like Irish hearts of oak and gain the victory.

So the battle it commence'd and the firing did begin
They wounded the captain's mate and killed two of his men
But our Irish boys were valiant and bold and our cannons loud did roar
And we killed ten of the pirate men and threw them overboard.

And the cries of women and children as in the hold they lay
And our captain and his gallant crew showed an Irish play
The captain's wife she came on board saying I'll soon end this strife
And with a pistol ball she took the pirate captain's life.

And it's to conclude and finish the truth I'll tell to you
We never lost a single man excepting one or two
And the pirate ship surrendered just at the break of day
And we brought her as a prisoner all to Amerikay.

Captain Thunderbolt

Words: trad. / Andy Irvine
Music: Andy Irvine

This song is a mystery to me. Who is Captain Thunderbolt? Apart from being a thorough Badness, he hints at a sub-plot in the penultimate verse. I have in vain looked up „Thunderbolt" in the telephone directory but his line appears to have died out … . Learned from the singing of Tom Moran, County Leitrim.

Dieses Lied verstehe ich nicht ganz. Wer ist Kapitän Thunderbolt? Abgesehen davon, daß er ein ausgemachter Bösewicht ist, gibt er sich in der vorletzten Strophe zu erkennen und legt gleich eine neue Fährte. Vergeblich habe ich im Telefonbuch unter „Thunderbolt" nachgesehen, seine Linie scheint ausgestorben zu sein … . Gelernt habe ich dieses Lied aus dem Repertoire von Tom Moran, County Leitrim.

cheeks like bloo - ming ro - ses this fair young maid re - plied. I'm
going to seek my fa - ther's sheep down by Lough Al - len side.

When Flora's flowery mantle it bedecked each field with pride
I met a comely damsel down by Lough Allen side

Good morning to you fair maid I modestly did say
What has you out so early or where are you going this way
Her cheeks like blooming roses this fair maid replied
I'm going to seek my father's sheep down by Lough Allen side.

I boldly stepped up to her and gave her a kiss
She says young man be civil on what do you mean by this
The grass is being mossy where we stood her feet from her did glide
And we both fell down together down by Lough Allen side.

Three times I kissed her ruby lips as we lay on the grass
And coming to herself again twas then she cried alas
Now you have had your will with me make me your lawful bride
Don't leave me here to mourn down by Lough Allen side.

Says I fair maid by easy from mourning now refrain
And we will speak of marriage sure when I come back again
And never let your courage fail no matter what betide
Untill I see your face again down by Lough Allen side.

So we kissed shook hands and parted an from her I did steer
I did not see her face again for over half a year
Walking down those flowery dells my love I chanced to spy
She was scarcely able for walk down by Logh Allen side.

I seemed to take no notice but continued on my way
As I turned my head around she desired for to stay
The tears like crystal fountains and they down her cheeks did slide
Saying don't forget the fall you gave down by Lough Allen side.

84

Fair maid your offer it is good and I do like it well
But I'm already promised and the truth to you I'll tell
Unto another fair maid that I mean to make my bride
She's wealthy grazier's daughter down by Lough Allen side.

Oh since you will not merry me pray tell me your name
That when my baby it is born I may call it the same
My name is Captain Thunderbolt and the same I'll never deny
I have good men at my command on yonder mountainside.

So we kissed shook hands and parted and then she went her way
And as I turned my head around these words I heard her say
This ought to be a warning now to all fair maids besides
To never trust a young man down by Lough Allen side.

The Dodger's Song

Words & Music: trad./ Dick Gaughan & Andy Irvine

My first influence was Woody Guthrie and this song was recorded by a group
Woody was with around 1940 called „The Almanac Singers". They were a
politically active bunch of musicians usually comprising Woody, Lee Hays,
Pete Seeger and Millard Lampell. Dick Gaughan and myself added a few extra
verses for good measure.

Mein erstes Vorbild war Woody Guthrie und dieses Lied wurde von einer Gruppe
aufgenommen, mit der Woody um 1940 herum unterwegs war. Sie hießen
„The Almanac Singers". Sie waren ein politisch aktiver Trupp von Musikern
wie Woody, Lee Hays, Pete Seeger und Millard Lampbell. Dick Gaughan und
ich haben ein paar Strophen hinzugefügt, um es abzurunden.

The politician is a dodger a well known dodger
Yes he is a dodger and I'm a dodger too
He'll meet you and treat you shake hands and gloat
Look out boys he's dodging for your vote.

Chorus:
O we're all a dodger a dodging dodging dodger
Yes we're all a dodger all the way through the world.

The lawyer is a dodger a well known dodger
Yes he is a dodger and I'm a dodger too
He'll plead your case and treat you as a friend
Look out boys he's easy for to bend.

The Clergyman's a dodger a well known dodger
Yes he is a dodger and I'm a dodger too
He'll preach you the Gospel and absolve you from sin
Meanwhile boys the money's rolling in.

The merchant is a dodger a well known dodger
Yes he is a dodger and I'm a dodger too
He'll sell you goods at double the price
And when you come to pay him you'll have to pay him twice.

The general is a dodger a well known dodger
Yes he is a dodger and I'm a dodger too
He'll pop into town he'll call for some wine
I'm afraid a great many the gallows will find.

The doctor is a dodger a well known dodger
Yes he is a dodger and I'm a dodger too
He'll treat you and care you for all you possess
And when you lay dying he'll rob you of the rest.

Băneasă's Green Glade

Words & Music: Andy Irvine

When I first arrived in Bucharest, I had nowhere to stay and after wandering
around, I found myself in Baneasa forest. Wound up staying there for months,
earning a living busking outside the zoo on Sundays. It was an idyllic spot.

Als ich zum ersten Mal nach Bukarest kam, wußte ich nicht, wo ich bleiben
sollte und gelangte nach einigem Umherstreifen in den Wald von Baneasa.
Am Ende blieb ich dort einige Monate und lebte von sonntäglicher Straßen-
musik vor dem Zoo. Es war ein idyllisches Fleckchen.

sweet scen - ted fire.___ In the still ear - ly mor - ning a cool gen - tle breeze, the e - cho of wood - peck - ers rings through the trees. We'd sit in our glade till the heat of the day, walk down to the zoo to sing, to play.

In Baneasa's green forest out under the trees
We'd lie on our backs we'd live at our ease
We'd wake in the morning at the first shafts of day
And watch the shy deer as they scampered away
We'd rise from our warm beds as the sun it got higher
And cook up our breakfast on a sweet scented fire
In the still early morning a cool gentle breeze
And the echo of woodpeckers rings through the trees
We'd sit in our glade till the heat of the day
Walk down to the zoo to sing and to play.

Well the money rolled in and the people looked on
When the hat was quite full we'd up and be gone
In Dimbovitsas tavern we spent money free
And drank to our friends whereever they may be
We'd talk of old times fond memories we'd trade
At dusk we'd walk home to Baneasa's green glade.

Sure to Be A Row

Words & Music: trad., arr. Andy Irvine

Learned from an old tape of the inimitable, much loved, late Willie Clancy.
Obviously of Music Hall origin and sung to the ubiquitous „Star of the County
Down" tune.

Kennengelernt habe ich dieses Lied durch eine alte Bandaufnahme mit dem
unnachahmlichen und beliebten, leider verstorbenen Willie Clancy. Offensichtlich stammt es aus den Music Halls. Gesungen wurde es zur allseits bekannten
Melodie von „Star of the County Down".

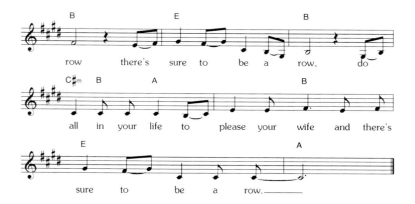

row there's sure to be a row, do all in your life to please your wife and there's sure to be a row.

I'm a poor unhappy married man I have an awful wife
Though I'll do everything she says yet still she plagues my life
Though I'll do everything thats right she'll find a fault somehow
And if I stay out late at night there's sure to be a row.

Chorus:

There's sure to be a row, there's sure to be a row
Do all in your life to please your wife and there's sure to be a row.

She wakes me in the morning in such a cruel way
She kicks me out upon the floor not a cross word dare I say
I have to wash my shirts and fronts, my socks also I vow
And if I don't wash hers as well there's sure to be a row.

(Chorus)

She's taken in a lodger now, he's single by and by
She says we must make room for him and I on the sofa lie
They eat the meat give me the bones it don't seem right somehow
And if I dare say one word there's sure to be a row.

I hand her up my wages after working all the week
I hand her up me wages still she has the cheek
To hand me twopence for myself and that I have to vow
That if I spend it all at once there's sure to be a row.

93

My Heart's Tonight In Ireland

Words & Music: Andy Irvine

A tribute to the memory of „Sweeney's Men", my first band. If days in the Balkans seem idyllic to me now, the earlier days travelling in the Sweeney Van seem like paradise! (They weren't at that time). The original Sweeney Van was a red VW that we paid about 17 £ for. The inside became permeated with rust and the smell of hungover bodies. Its usual load would be Eamonn O'Doherty (manager), his wife Barbara (co-driver), Johnny Moynihan (the only band member with a semblance of knowledge of motor-vehicles and that little enough, God knows), Joe Dolan (band member with a hatred for motor vehicles that didn't go), Andy Irvine (somewhere in between), Muriel Geraghty (my girlfriend), Annie Briggs (Moynihan's girlfriend) and at different times, many's another. It wasn't so much a Van as a travelling doss-house but it had a terrible thirst for oil which seemed to spurt out of a dozen orifices underneath. Johnny came up to me one day and said with a smirk of satisfaction: „Andy, I've found a place where they sell 'used' oil!" That proved to be the beginning of the end. The Van rejected the notion of using other vehicles' cast off, thin, black lubricant and after demanding a refill very 22 1/2 miles, finally shuddered to a halt outside Craughwell in County Galway. It was last heard of being used as a chicken coop which pleased us all greatly and would have pleased poor „Mad Sweeney" after whom we were named. Here's to all who travelled with Sweeney, to all the great people we met along the way, to the farmers on whose potato fields we relied, and most of all to the great Willie Clancy, his pipes and his friendly face.

Eine Huldigung an „Sweeney's Men", meine erste Band. Wenn die Zeit auf dem Balkan mir heute idyllisch vorkommt, so waren die früheren Zeiten, als wir in Sweeney's Van unterwegs waren, das Paradies (damals kam uns das allerdings nicht so vor). Sweeney's Van war ein roter VW-Bus, für den wir etwa 17 £ bezahlt hatten. Sein Inneres war rostüberzogen und von den Ausdünstungen seiner verkaterten Insassen durchdrungen. Die übliche Ladung bestand aus Eamonn O'Doherty (Manager), seiner Frau Barbara (Beifahrerin), Johnny Moynihan (Bandmitglied; der einzige mit halbwegs Ahnung von Motoren), Joe Dolan (Bandmitglied; er hasste Motoren, die nicht liefen), Andy Irvine (irgendwo dazwischen), Muriel Geraghty (meine Freundin), Annie Briggs (Moynihans Freundin) und zuweilen viele andere. Es war weniger ein Van, als eine fahrende Absteige, mit einem unstillbaren Durst nach Öl, das er aus zahlreichen Öffnungen wieder verlor. Eine Tages kam Johnny mit einem zufriedenen Grinsen zu mir: „Andy, ich habe eine Stelle gefunden, wo sie 'gebrauchtes' Öl verkaufen!" Das war der Anfang vom Ende. Der Van weigerte sich, den Abfall anderer Fahrzeuge, eine dünne, schwarze Schmiere, anzunehmen. Alle 22 1/2 Meilen verlangte er Nachschub und blieb außerhalb von Craughwell im

County Galway schließlich stotternd stehen. Das letzte, was wir über ihn hör-
ten war, daß er als Hühnerstall benutzt wurde. Das gefiel nicht nur uns, es
hätte auch „Mad Sweeney", nach dem wir uns nannten, viel Freude bereitet.
Auf alle, die mit Sweeney unterwegs waren, auf die tollen Leute, die wir auf
der Reise trafen, die Farmer, auf deren Kartoffelfelder wir uns verlassen konn-
ten und vor allem auf die Erinnerung an den großen Willie Clancy, seine Pipes
und sein sympathisches Gesicht.

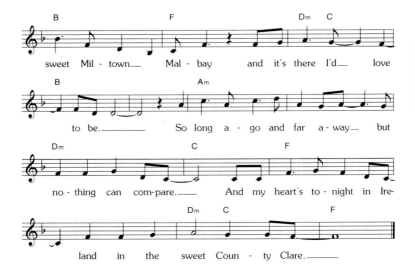

sweet Mil - town__ Mal - bay and it's there I'd__ love
to be.____ So long a - go and far a - way__ but
no - thing can com-pare.____ And my heart's to - night in Ireland in the sweet Coun - ty Clare.____

In the town of Scariff the sun was shining in the sky
When Willie Clancy played his pipes
And the tears welled in my eyes
Many years have passed and gone
Since the times we had there
But my heart's tonight in Ireland
In the sweet County Clare.

My heart tonight is far across the rolling sea
In the sweet Miltown Malbay it's there I'd love to be
So long ago and far away but nothing can compare
My heart's tonight in Ireland
In the sweet County Clare.

That august in Kilrush when the rain was lashing down
And our hotel was that haybarn
On the outskirts of town
We were all sick and feverish
And Dolan had the flu
But Johnny produced some Whiskey
And the sun came smiling through.

Those nights in Sixmilebridge
When the songs and music flowed
And when it came to closing time
Sure the lights were turned down low
And the sergeant from Kilkishen
He would by us all one more
And we never left that pub before
The clock was striking four.

Lahinch and Ennistymon, Liscannor and Kilkee
But the best of all was Miltown
When the music flowed so free
Willie Clancy and the County Clare
I'm ever in your debt
For the sights and sounds of yesterday
Are shining memories yet.

My heart tonight is far across the rolling sea
In the sweet Miltown Malbay it's there I'd love to be
So long ago and far away but nothing can compare
My heart's tonight in Ireland
In the sweet County Clare.

Outro

Back in the early sixties, life seemed to be timeless. Looking back, each and every day seems to have been spent in Maureen and Paddy O'Donoghue's Godsend of a pub in Merrion Row, Dublin.

Godsend, I say and mean it on every level. Not only would you be sure, seven days a week, of the presence of your friends, music and the crack, countless pints, the payment for which was often delayed or even overlooked by Paddy's kindness but if you were able to struggle from the bed in the morning (and I only lived across the road), you would, more than likely be invited for a cup of tea, a bowl of soup, a hearty sandwich and an enquiry into your financial straits by Maureen.

Without all this, life would have been unimaginable as there was very little money in our kind of music then. Then came the so-called „Ballad Boom". Ballad sessions were all the rage and I found myself in a trio called „Sweeney's Men". I don't think we were ever as popular as some of the others. We still hung on to an idealistic approach which precluded any form of slickness or „strokeyness" - as they used to call it. We had our faithful following alright, but they wouldn't have jammed „The Embankment". I got an itch for the road ... Me and the other Sweeney's recorded an album and I headed off in the general direction of Istanbul.

It was 1968 and years later looking back, I came to realise that that year was something unusual. Either everybody was on the road, going somewhere or they were doing something else strange. Why I was travelling, I don't know. Hitching around the Balkans, sleeping in fields, stared at by the natives, eking out my money as far as it would go, seeing an unusual name on the map and going to see what is was like. I became wonderfully thin after a year and a half of that and decided to head home and see what the score was. Back in Dublin things had change quite a lot. Or maybe I had. O'Donoghues was not the same. It had become world famous.

Andy Irvine

In den frühen sechziger Jahren schien das Leben endlos zu sein. Rückblickend kommt es mir vor, als hätte ich Tag für Tag in Maureen und Paddy O'Donoghues Gottesgabe eines Pubs in der Dubliner Merrion Row verbracht.

Gottesgabe meine ich in jeder Beziehung. Sieben Tage die Woche konntest Du sicher sein, hier all Deine Freunde zu treffen, es gab gute Musik, gute Stimmung und zahllose Biere, deren Bezahlung Paddy in seiner Freundlichkeit häufig erst viel später verlangte oder einfach übersah. Wenn Du dann doch in der Lage warst, Dich am nächsten Morgen aus dem Bett zu kämpfen (und ich wohnte nur quer über die Straße), war es mehr als wahrscheinlich, daß Du von Maureen zu einer Tasse Tee, einem Teller Suppe, einem herzhaften Sandwich und einer Erörterung Deiner finanziellen Schwierigkeiten eingeladen wurdest. Ohne all dies wäre das Leben buchstäblich unvorstellbar gewesen, denn es gab mit unserer Musik nicht viel zu verdienen. Dann kam der sogenannte „Balladen-Boom". Sessions und das Singen waren der letzte Schrei und ich befand mich auf einmal in einem Trio namens „Sweeney's Men". Ich glaube nicht, daß wir je so populär waren wie manch andere. Wir waren immer noch Anhänger einer idealistischen Herangehensweise an die Musik und lehnten jede Form von Schmalz oder „Ruck-Zuck-Gesang" ab, wie man das damals nannte. Wir hatten unsere treue Gefolgschaft, ganz klar, aber die wäre nie für eine Session ins „The Embankment"* gekommen. Ich bekam Lust aufs Reisen ... .

Wir nahmen mit den Sweeneys eine Schallplatte auf, und dann fuhr ich los in Richtung Istanbul.

Das war 1968 und rückblickend fällt mir auf, wie außergewöhnlich dieses Jahr war. Entweder befand sich jeder auf Reisen, um irgendwohin zu kommen, oder er machte sonst etwas Verrücktes. Warum ich unterwegs war, weiß ich nicht. Ich trampte durch den Balkan, schlief auf Feldern, wurde von Einheimischen bestaunt, schlug mich mit meinem Geld so weit durch, wie es irgend ging, und wenn ich einen ungewöhnlichen Namen auf der Landkarte fand, fuhr ich an den Ort, um herauszufinden, wie es dort aussah. Nach anderthalb Jahren war ich wunderbar dünn geworden und ich beschloß, nach Hause zu fahren und zu sehen, wie die Dinge dort lagen. In Dublin war alles anders geworden. Oder vielleicht hatte ich mich auch verändert. O'Donoghue's war nicht mehr so, wie ich es kannte. Es war weltberühmt geworden.

Andy Irvine

*Nobel-Club für schnulzige Balladensänger in Dublin (Anm. d. Übers.).

Andy Irvine

The Works / Die Werke

West Coast Of Clare. Copyright © by Andy Irvine & Heupferd Musik Verlag (f. Germany, Austria & Switzerland). Rec.: „Planxty" (Polydor 2383-186). Rec. & rel. 1972. CD: Shanachie 79009. Andy Irvine (voc., mandolin), Donal Lunny (voc., bouz.), Christy Moore (guit.), Liam O'Flynn (tin whistle).

Arthur MacBride. Copyright © by Andy Irvine. Rec.: „Planxty" (Polydor 2383-186). Rec. & rel. 1972. CD: Shanachie 79009. Andy Irvine (voc., mandola), Donal Lunny (voc., bouz.), Christy Moore (voc., guit.), Liam O'Flynn (uilleann pipes).

Pat Reilly. Copyright © by Andy Irvine. Rec.: „Planxty - The Well Below The Valley" (Polydor 283232). Rec. & rel. 1973. CD: Shanachie 79010. Andy Irvine (voc., mandolin), Donal Lunny (bouz.), Liam O'Flynn (tin whistle).

Time Will Cure Me. Copyright © by Andy Irvine & Mews Music. Rec.: „Planxty - The Well Below The Valley" (Polydor 283232). Rec. & rel. 1973. CD: Shanachie 79010. Andy Irvine (voc., mandola), Donal Lunny (guit.), Christy Moore (harmonium), Liam O'Flynn (tin whistle).

Plains Of Kildare. Copyright © by Andy Irvine & Mulligan Music. Rec.: „Andy Irvine & Paul Brady" (Mulligan LUN 008). Rec. & rel. 1976. Andy Irvine (voc., bouz., mandolin), Paul Brady (voc., guit.), Donal Lunny (guit.), Kevin Burke (fiddle). CD: „Celtic Folk Festival (Munich Records MRCD 183). Andy Irvine (voc., bouz.), Gerry O'Beirne (guit.).

Bonny Woodhall. Copyright © by Andy Irvine & Mulligan Music. Rec.: „Andy Irvine & Paul Brady" (Mulligan LUN 008). Rec. & rel. 1976. Andy Irvine (voc., bouz.), Paul Brady (cittern, tin whistle, harmonium), Donal Lunny (guit.). Rec.:"The 4th Irish Folk Festival On The Road" (Intercord INT 180.038). Rec. & rel. 1977; CD: Wundertüte TÜT 72.74771-2. Rel. 1993. Andy Irvine (voc., bouz.), Mick Hanly (voc., guit).

Martinmas Time. Copyright © by Andy Irvine & Mulligan Music. Rec.: „Andy Irvine & Paul Brady" (Mulligan LUN 008). Rec. & rel. 1976. Andy Irvine (voc., hurdy gurdy, mandolin), Paul Brady (voc., guit., harmonium, whistle), Donal Lunny (voc., guit., bouz.), Kevin Burke (fiddle).

Autumn Gold. Copyright © by Andy Irvine & Mulligan Music. Rec.: Andy Irvine & Paul Brady" (Mulligan LUN 008). Rec. & rel. 1976. Andy Irvine (voc., mandola), Donal Lunny (guit.).

The Rambling Siúler. Copyright © by Andy Irvine & Mild Music. Rec.: „Planxty - After The Break" (Tara 3001). Rec. & rel. 1979; CD: Tara 3001. Andy Irvine (voc., mandola), Donal Lunny (bouz.), Christy Moore (guit.), Liam O'Flynn (whistle), Matt Molloy (whistle).

You Rambling Boys Of Pleasure. Copyright © by Andy Irvine & Mild Music Rec.:„Planxty - After The Break" (Tara 3001). Rec. & rel. 1979; CD: Tara 3001. Andy Irvine (voc., mandola, hurdy gurdy), Donal Lunny (guit.), Christy Moore (harmonium), Liam O'Flynn (whistle), Matt Molloy (whistle).

Smeceno Horo. Copyright © by Andy Irvine & Mild Music. Rec.: „Planxty - After The

Break" (Tara 3001). Rec. & rel. 1979; CD: Tara 3001. Andy Irvine (bouz.), Donal Lunny (bouz.), Christy Moore (bodhrán), Liam O'Flynn (whistle, uilleann pipes), Mat Molloy (flute).

Roger O'Hehir. Copyright © by Andy Irvine & Mild Music. Rec.: „Planxty - The Woman I Loved So Well" (Tara 3005). Rec. & rel. 1980; CD: Tara 3005. Andy Irvine (voc., bouz.), Donal Lunny (keyboards, bouz.), Christy Moore (guit.), Liam O'Flynn (whistle, uilleann pipes), Noel Hill (concertina), Tony Linnane (fiddle).

Kellswater. Copyright © by Andy Irvine & Mild Music. Rec.: „Planxty - The Woman I Loved So Well" (Tara 3005). Rec. & rel. 1980; CD: Tara 3005. Andy Irvine (voc., bouz.), Donal Lunny (guit., keyboards), Liam O'Flynn (low whistle), Bill Whelan (fender rhodes).

Johnny Of Brady's Lea. Copyright © by Andy Irvine & Mild Music. Rec.: „Planxty - The Woman I Loved So Well" (Tara 3005). Rec. & rel. 1980; CD: Tara 3005. Andy Irvine (voc., bouz.), Donal Lunny (keyboards, bouz.), Christy Moore (guit.), Liam O'Flynn (whistle, uilleann pipes), Noel Hill (concertina), Tony Linnane (fiddle).

Thousands Are Sailing. Copyright © by Andy Irvine & Heupferd Musik (f. Germany, Austria & Switzerland). Rec.: „Folk Friends 2" (Folk Freak FF 403003). Rec. & rel. 1980. CD: Wundertüte TÜT 72.150. Rel. 1990. Andy Irvine (voc., bouz.), Dick Gaughan (guit.). Rec.: „Planxty - Words & Music" (WEA 24-0101-1). Rec. & rel. 1982. CD: Shanachie 79035. Andy Irvine (voc., bouz.), Donal Lunny (keyboards, guit.), Liam O'Flynn (uilleann pipes).

Napoleon Bonaparte. Copyright © by Andy Irvine & Mild Music. Rec.: „High Kings Of Tara" (Tara 3003). Rec. 1979, rel. 1980. Andy Irvine (voc., bouz., harmonica), Donal Lunny (voc., guit.), Christy Moore (voc., guit.), Liam O'Flynn (uilleann pipes), Matt Molloy (flute).

General Munroe. Copyright © by Andy Irvine & Mild Music. Rec.: „High Kings Of Tara" (Tara 3003). Rec. 1979, rel. 1980. Andy Irvine (voc., bouz., harmonica), Donal Lunny (voc., guit.).

Farewell To Old Ireland. Copyright © by Andy Irvine & Heupferd Musik Verlag (f. Germany, Austria & Switzerland). Rec.: „Andy Irvine - Rainy Sundays ... Windy Dreams" (Tara 3002). Rec. & rel. 1980; CD: Wundertüte TÜT 72.141, rel. 1989. Andy Irvine (voc., mandolas, harmonica), Donal Lunny (voc., bouz.), Paul Brady (guit.), Frankie Gavin (fiddle), Rick Epping (harmonica).

Edward Conners. Copyright © by Andy Irvine & Heupferd Musik Verlag (f. Germany, Austria & Switzerland). Rec.: „Andy Irvine - Rainy Sundays ... Windy Dreams" (Tara 3002). Rec. & rel. 1980; CD: Wundertüte TÜT 72.141, rel. 1989. Andy Irvine (voc., bouz.), Donal Lunny (harmonium), Frankie Gavin (fiddle).

The Longford Weaver. Copyright © by Andy Irvine & Heupferd Musik Verlag (f. Germany, Austria & Switzerland). Rec.: „The 5th Irish Folk Festival" (Intercord INT 180.046); CD: Wundertüte TÜT 72.74781-2, rel. 1993. Andy Irvine (voc., hurdy gurdy, harmonica), Mick Hanly (guit.). Rec.: „Andy Irvine - Rainy Sundays ... Windy Dreams" (Tara 3002). Rec. & rel. 1980; CD: Wundertüte TÜT 72.141, rel. 1989. Andy Irvine (voc., hurdy gurdy, harmonica), Frankie Gavin (viola), Rick Epping (harmonica).

Farewell To Ballymoney. Copyright © by Andy Irvine & Heupferd Musik Verlag (f. Germany, Austria & Switzerland). Rec.: „Andy Irvine - Rainy Sundays ... Windy Dreams"

(Tara 3002). Rec. & rel. 1980; CD: Wundertüte TÜT 72.141, rel. 1989. Andy Irvine (voc., mandola), Donal Lunny (guit.), Paul Brady (piano).

Romanian Song (Blood And Gold). Copyright © by Andy Irvine & Heupferd Musik Verlag (f. Germany, Austria & Switzerland). Rec.: „Andy Irvine - Rainy Sundays ... Windy Dreams" (Tara 3002). Rec. & rel. 1980; CD: Wundertüte TÜT 72.141, rel. 1989. „Magic Women Of Ireland" Vive La Difference VLDCD 29925, rel. 1998. Andy Irvine (bouz.), Lucienne Purcell (voc.), Donal Lunny (10 string bouz.), Frankie Gavin (fiddles), Rick Epping (accordion).

King Bore And The Sandman. Copyright © by Andy Irvine & Heupferd Musik Verlag (f. Germany, Austria & Switzerland). Rec.: „Andy Irvine - Rainy Sundays ... Windy Dreams" (Tara 3002). Rec. & rel. 1980; CD: Wundertüte TÜT 72.141, rel. 1989. „Magic Irish Inspirations" Vive La Difference VLDCD 20022, rel. 2002. Andy Irvine (voc., mandolins), Donal Lunny (bouz. panpipes, vocal-effects).

Rainy Sundays. Copyright © by Andy Irvine & Heupferd Musik Verlag (f. Germany, Austria & Switzerland). Rec.: „Andy Irvine - Rainy Sundays ... Windy Dreams" (Tara 3002). Rec. & rel. 1980; CD: Wundertüte TÜT 72.141, rel. 1989. „Magic Irish Romances" Vive La Difference VLDCD 29924, rel. 1998. Andy Irvine (voc., bouz.), Donal Lunny (bouz.), Paul Barett (keyboards), Garvan Gallagher (e-bass), Keith Donald (sopr.-sax.).

Willy O'Winsbury. Copyright © by Andy Irvine & Heupferd Musik Verlag (f. Germany, Austria & Switzerland). Rec.: „Sweeney's Men" (Transatlantic TRA 170). Rec. & rel. 1968. Andy Irvine (voc., guit.).

Creggan White Hare. Copyright © by Andy Irvine & Heupferd Musik Verlag (f. Germany, Austria & Switzerland). Rec.: „Dick Gaugan & Andy Irvine - Parallel Lines" (Folk Freak FF 40.4007). Rec. 1981, rel. 1982; CD: Wundertüte TÜT 72.4007, rel. 1988. Andy Irvine (voc., bouz., harmonica), Dick Gaughan (guit.), Nollaigh Ni Chathasaigh (fiddle). CD: „Celtic Folk Festival" (Munich Records MRCD 183). Andy Irvine (voc., bouz. harmonica), Gerry O'Beirne (guit.).

At Twenty-One. Copyright © by Andy Irvine & Heupferd Musik Verlag (f. Germany, Austria & Switzerland). Rec.: „Dick Gaugan & Andy Irvine - Parallel Lines" (Folk Freak FF 40.4007). Rec. 1981, rel. 1982; CD: Wundertüte TÜT 72.4007, rel. 1988. „Magic Irish Roots" Vive La Difference VLDCD 20023, rel. 2002. Andy Irvine (voc., mandola), Dick Gaughan (guit.), Judith Jaenicke (flute). Bob Lenox (fender rhodes).

Captain Colston. Copyright © by Andy Irvine & Heupferd Musik Verlag (f. Germany, Austria & Switzerland). Rec.: „Dick Gaugan & Andy Irvine - Parallel Lines" (Folk Freak FF 40.4007). Rec. 1981, rel. 1982; CD: Wundertüte TÜT 72.4007, rel. 1988. Andy Irvine (voc., mandolins, harmonica), Dick Gaughan (guit.), Nollaigh Ni Chathasaigh (fiddle).

Captain Thunderbolt. Copyright © by Andy Irvine & Heupferd Musik Verlag (f. Germany, Austria & Switzerland). Rec.: „Dick Gaugan & Andy Irvine - Parallel Lines" (Folk Freak FF 40.4007). Rec. 1981, rel. 1982; CD: Wundertüte TÜT 72.4007, rel. 1988. „Magic Irish Voices" Vive La Difference VLDCD 29923, rel. 1998. Andy Irvine (voc., bouz.), Dick Gaughan (guit.).

The Dodger's Song. Copyright © by Andy Irvine & Heupferd Musik Verlag (f. Germany, Austria & Switzerland). Rec.: „Dick Gaugan & Andy Irvine - Parallel Lines" (Folk Freak FF 40.4007). Rec. 1981, rel. 1982; CD: Wundertüte TÜT 72.4007, rel. 1988.

103

Andy Irvine (voc., bouz., harmonica, mandolin), Dick Gaughan (voc., e-bass, guit).

Baneasa's Green Glade. Copyright © by Andy Irvine & Heupferd Musik Verlag (f. Germany, Austria & Switzerland). Rec.: „Planxty - Cold Blow And The Rainy Night" (Polydor 2383301). Rec. & rel. 1974. CD: Shanachie 79011. Andy Irvine (voc., mandola), Donal Lunny (bouz.), Christy Moore (harmonium). „Mozaik - Live From The Powerhouse" (Hummingbird Records HBCD 0036). Rec. 2002, rel. 2004. Andy Irvine (voc., bouz.), Donal Lunny (guit.), Rens van der Zalm (mandolin), Nikola Parov (gadulka).

Sure To Be A Row. Copyright © by Andy Irvine & Heupferd Musik Verlag (f. Germany, Austria & Switzerland). Rec.: „The Gathering" (Greenhays GR 705). Rec. & rel. 1977. Andy Irvine (voc., bouz.), Paul Brady (guit., whistles).

My Heart's Tonight In Ireland. Copyright © by Andy Irvine & Heupferd Musik Verlag (f. Germany, Austria & Switzerland). Rec.: „Common Ground - Voices Of Modern Irish Music" (EMI premier 724383769124). Rec. & rel. 1996. Andy Irvine (voc.,bouz.), Donal Lunny (bass bodhran), Rens van der Zalm (mandolin), David Hayes (keyboards), Eoin O'Neill (guit., bass), Rita Connolly (backing voc.). „Andy Irvine - Rain On The Roof" CD AK 1, Rec. & rel. 1996. Andy Irvine (voc., mandolins). „Mozaik - Live From The Powerhouse" (Hummingbird Records HBCD 0036). Rec. 2002, rel. 2004. Andy Irvine (voc., bouz.), Donal Lunny (voc., guit.), Bruce Molsky (fiddle), Rens van der Zalm (mandolin, voc.), Nikola Parov (whistle).

Discography Andy Irvine

Andy Irvine Albums: „Andy Irvine & Paul Brady" (Mulligan LP LUN 008). „Andy Irvine - Rainy Sundays ... Windy Dreams" (Wundertüte CD 72.141). Andy Irvine & Dick Gaughan - Parallel Lines" (Wundertüte CD 72.4007). „Andy Irvine - Rude Awakening" (Green Linnet GLCD 11143). „Andy Irvine & Davey Spillane - East Wind" (Tara CD 3027). „Andy Irvine - Rain On The Roof" (CD AK 1). „Andy Irvine - Way Out Yonder" (CD AK 2).

Andy Irvine & Sweeney's Men: „Sweeney's Men - 1968" (Transatlantic TRA 170).

Andy Irvine & Planxty: „Christy Moore - Prosperous" (Tara CD 2008). „Planxty - Planxty" (Shanachie CD 79010). „Planxty - The Well Below The Valley" (Shanachie CD 79010). „Planxty - Cold Blow The Rainy Night" (Shanachie CD 79011). „Planxty - After The Break" (Tara CD 3001). „Planxty - The Woman I Loved So Well" (Tara CD 3001). „Planxty - Words & Music" (Shanachie CD 79035).

Andy Irvine & Patrick Street: „Patrick Street - Patrick Street" (Green Linnet GLCD 1071). „Patrick Street - No. 2" (Green Linnet GLCD 1088). „Patrick Street - Irish Times" (Green Linnet GLCD 1105). „Patrick Street - All In Good Time" (Green Linnet GLCD 1125). „Patrick Street - Corner Boys" (Green Linnet GLCD 1160). „Patrick Street - Made In Cork" (Green Linnet GLCD 1184). „Patrick Street - Live From Patrick

Street" (Green Linnet GLCD 1194). „Patrick Street - Compendium" (Green Linnet GLCD 1207). „Patrick Street - Street Life" (Green Linnet GLCD 1222). „Patrick Street - On The Fly" (Loftus Music).

Andy Irvine & Mozaik: „Andy Irvine & Donal Lunny's Mozaik - Live From The Power-house" (Mozaik Rec. MOZCD01). Andy Irvine & Donal Lunny's Mozaik - Changing Trains" (Mozaik Rec. MOZCD02).

Those were the days
Andy Irvine & Paul Brady 1978
(Photo: Michael Krebs)

For more information visit
www.andyirvine.com

Das Klingt Gut!
Musik der Welt im Netz

Acoustic Music | Derroll Adams | Alla Turca
Anti-Hits | Balladen | Bastardmusik | Barden
Böhmische Harfe | Bordun | Pit Budde | Robert Burns
Guy Carawan | Cochise | Tom Daun | Ethnobeats
Flamenco | Folkaffairs | Folk Friends | Folkjazz
Folkmusic | Folkrock | Folksong | Dick Gaughan
Mike Hanrahan | Harfenflocken | Harfissimo | Havana
Hobomusic | Bobby Holcomb | Annie Humphrey
Hurdy Gurdy | Indian Summer Sounds | Andy Irvine
Jams | Jazz | Wizz Jones | Klassikfolk | Kurt Klose
Jorge La Guardia | Lady's Voice | La Rotta | Latinpop
Latinjazz | Latinrap | Andreas Lieberg | Lovesongs
Denise M'Baye | Magic Irish Music | Magic Southsea
Migration & Musik | Native American Music | Noten
Protestsong | Rüdiger Oppermann | Marc Robine
Rootsmusic | Samba | Salsa | Son | Songbooks
Song Bücherei | Songwriter | Andy M. Stewart
Wolfgang Stute | Summit | Tierra | Trio Grande
Can Tufan | Jake Walton | Worldmusic

www.heupferd-musik.de

Lightning Source UK Ltd.
Milton Keynes UK
UKOW02f2322241016
286024UK00001B/68/P